The raft

This is the cliff top.

Can you see the van?

It is next to some rocks.

Can you see a cross?

Can you see some more distant things?

Everything is still.

Where are Eggin, the Slinx and the fuzzbuzzes?

Write

The van is still on the cliff top.

The band are not there.

This is where they are!
It is the band's very first
visit to the sands.
Everyone just left the van and
went dashing down the cliff.
Now they are having smashing fun.
Can you see what they are doing?

Draw some of the things the band are doing.
Write
Everyone plays on the sands.

Because this is the first visit,
everything is puzzling.
What are things called?
One of the fuzzbuzzes goes across
to Eggin and asks,
'What is this big blue
pond called?'
Eggin asks the Slinx for the map so
he can read the words on it.
Some of them are big words and
Eggin has to do his best.
At last he does it.
'It's called the Atlantic Pond!' he
tells the little one.
And from then on, that is what
everyone called it.

In the end Eggin tells everyone
that they still have a lot to do.
'Yes,' nods the Slinx. 'The sun
is setting. We must not get stuck
down at the bottom of this cliff in
pitch blackness. There is a mass
of things to do!'
'If we are going to get rich we
must get cracking!' Eggin tells
them.
They are all a bit sad, but they
have to admit that Eggin is
correct.
They set off, back up the steps
that are cut into the cliff.

Write
The band must stop playing.
Draw them going back up the cliff.

9

Eggin switches on the lamps from the van.
Now they can see what they are doing.
Everyone has a job to do.
Eggin puts the tent up.
The fuzzbuzzes unpack the van and stack everything next to the tent.
The Slinx gets dinner ready.

Draw the band getting on with the jobs.
Write
The band get the camp ready.
There is lots to do.

They have all had second helpings
of dinner from the big black pot.
They cannot eat one more thing.
They are happy and content.
'What a splendid dinner! What did
you put in it?' Eggin asks.
'A bit of everything,' admits the
Slinx.
The fuzzbuzzes ask him if he will
do all the dinners.
The Slinx promises that he will
if they eat everything up.
Eggin pulls a clock out of his bag.
He sets it for ten to six.
'We must all go to bed now,' he
tells them. 'We must get up with
the sun. Then we can test the
raft.'

Write

Everyone is full up.
They are ready for bed.

DING-A-LING-A-LING!
What a shock!
The bells on the clock have
everyone jumping out of bed.
But now they have had a good sleep,
and they are ready to get on with
the job.

> **Draw the clock going off.**
> **Write**
> Everyone jumps out of bed.

The Slinx goes across to the top of the cliff.

He is thinking of a method for getting the raft to the bottom of the cliff.

It is very difficult.

The raft is so big.

One slip, and it will go tumbling down and smash to bits.

It is a baffling problem.

Just then, Eggin comes across.

The Slinx asks him what he thinks.

Eggin thinks for a bit, but he cannot help.

They sit down on the cliff top.

They are in a fix.

If they cannot get the raft down they will have to give up.

Now the fuzzbuzzes come across.
'What's the problem?' they ask.
Eggin tells them.
They all sit down on the cliff top.
They are in a fix.
But Eggin will not give up.
He tells them that they must sit there until someone comes up with a practical plan for getting the raft down to the sands.
They sit and sit and sit.
The fuzzbuzzes are not very good at thinking.
Some of them nod off.

Draw the band on the cliff top.
Write
The band has to think of a plan.
Some of them are not very
good at thinking.

The band are
still sitting there.
Everyone is glum.
Not one of them can
think of a plan.
Then Eggin jumps up.
He does a little jig.
He stretches out his
hand.
He yells out
'Can you see that?'

'So what?' grunts the Slinx.

'How does that help us?'

Eggin jumps up and down.

'You are a nitwit!' he yells.

'The Atlantic Pond has come in.

It's come across the sand and up to

the cliff! All we have to do is

push the raft off the cliff top.

It will have a soft landing!'

Now the Slinx jumps up.

'Brilliant!' he yells.

'Let's get on with it!'

They all rush off to get the raft.

Draw the Atlantic coming in.
Write
The Atlantic has come in.
The band rush off to get the raft.

The raft is a big, solid lump.
It is a difficult job to get it
across to the cliff top.
The band have to
  push and pull,
  drag and yank,
  tug and lug,
  press and thrust
to get it there.
But in the end they do it.
Now they can push it off the top.
'1, 2, 3,' yells the Slinx. 'PUSH!'
At first the raft just tilts a bit.
'MORE!' yells the Slinx.
Everyone gives one last, big push.
That does it.
The raft goes tumbling down.

Draw the raft tumbling down.

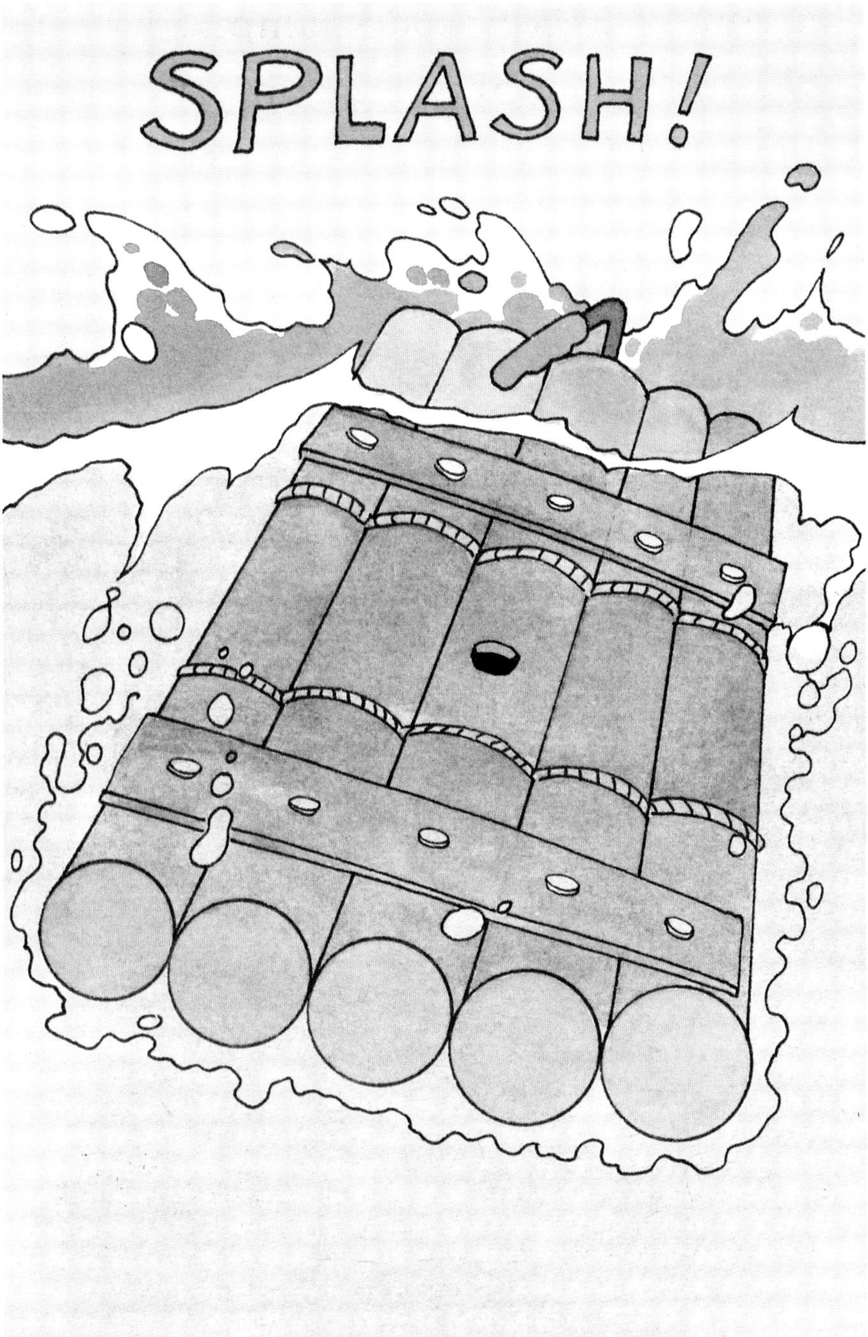
SPLASH!

Everyone dashes to the cliff top to
see what is happening.
They cannot see the raft.
The Atlantic is flat and level.
There is nothing there!
Ten seconds pass, then ten more.
Still nothing happens.
The Slinx is very upset.
His raft has sunk!
Now they have had it!

**Draw the flat and level
Atlantic.**
Write
The raft goes tumbling into the
Atlantic.
But now there's nothing there.

Then,

　Splosh! Glug! Slosh!

The raft pops up!

It bobs up and down on the blue
Atlantic.

They all clap and yell.

Then they hug the Slinx and pat him
on the back.

'Come on, then,' they yell. 'Let's
go on a trip!'

'Just a sec.,' begs the Slinx,

'There's something to get first.'

And he dashes back to the van.

**Draw the raft bobbing up and
down on the blue Atlantic.**
Write
The raft comes up at last.
It does not sink.

The rest of the band go down the rock steps to the bottom of the cliff.

Eggin goes paddling out to fetch the raft.

The raft has drifted out of his depth, so he has to swim the last bit.

He pulls the raft back, and the fuzzbuzzes jump on.

Then there is a yell.

'Do not set off yet!'

The Slinx comes dashing down
the steps.
Can you see him?
The Slinx jumps on the raft.
Everyone is giggling.
They think that the Slinx's
outfit is brilliant.
'Come on, men!' the Slinx yells.
'We will go off on a test trip.'
Paddling a raft is very difficult,
and the band gets into a big mess.

Draw the Slinx.
Write
The Slinx loves dressing up.

First, the raft goes into a spin.
Next, it hits a rock.
Then, the Slinx goes in!
Everyone gets dripping wet,
but in the end they do it!
Now the raft goes well.

1 Write down 3 things the band do on the sands. (5)

2 Why does Eggin think the band must go back up the cliff? (8)

3 How can they see to do all the jobs? (10)

4 What does the Slinx put into the dinner? (12)

5 What is a problem? (16)

6 What happens next, so that they can get the raft down without smashing it? (21)

7 At first, what happens to the raft? (22)

8 The Slinx dresses up. What colour are
      his patch
      his boots
      and his hat? (28)